Being Love

by Ron Bracale

Being Love

Written from 2007-07-06 to 2003-11-18

©2013 Ronald A. Bracale

All Rights Reserved

ISBN: 978-1-941090-00-8

Published by

Enlightening Treasures

Conneaut, OH

Enlightening Thoughts

Vol. 1: Knowledge of Love

Vol. 2: Healing Love

Vol. 3: Spiritual Love

Vol. 4: True Love

Vol. 5: Being Love

Open your heart and experience these transformative meditations. We live within our paradigm of reality and it is a continually metamorphosing world view. These meditations are the gift of the wisdom of my life's journey and my deep meditative contemplation. Let these Enlightening Thoughts stir you to make conscious what you truly know in your Heart and expand your perceived reality. A whole new existence is awaiting us with feelings of wonderment and joy.

We live and love: that is profound and amazing; yet, it also incites us with a deep yearning to know and understand this journey in the fullest manner possible. Words can only hint at truth and each person must come to Know from their own unique point of view. These words hold keys; yet, you must open the doors to your own inner Wisdom as you walk your life. The Divine Mystery of Creation is only accessible through direct experience. I share these gifts with my love.

May we grow together toward a bright future.

May you 'Be Love' during your Life's Journey.

Table of Contents

1: QUESTIONS 1
    The Call? 2
    Satisfaction? 6
    Treasures? 9
    Future Generations? 11
    Fierce Love? 15
    Desire and Aversion? 17
    Death? 19
    Relationships? 21
    Are we True? 23
    Sharing? 24
    Inner Life? 25
    Freedom? 27
    Releasing? 31
    Perspective? 33

2: GLOWING ELIXIR 35
    Transformations 36
    Spirit Fight 39
    Thousands of possibilities 40
    Sitting Still 41
    Destiny 42
    No Form 43
    Creation Balance 44
    Elixir 45
    cutting puppet strings 46
    Ancient Pueblo Flute 47
    The Primal Imprint 48

3: LEARNING DEEPER LOVE 50
    Opening 51

    Teacher 52
    always Loving deeper 53
    I ask myself 55
    Fools in Paradise 57
    My Soul 59
    Tickle my Soul 61
    Fully Human 63
    Bamboo 64

4: CHANGES 67
    Our Mother 68
    Commentary on Balance 69
    Divine Feminine 71
    Silver and Gold 72
    Heart Blessings 74
    Changing Balances 75
    Soul Memory 76
    What are we? 77
    Listening to the Heart 78

5: NONDUALISTIC REALITY 79
    Montheism 80
    Multicolor reality 84
    slow down 89
    all we can do 90
    Hungry Souls 91
    Riches 92
    mortal sorrows 93
    Wordcraft 94
    Ecological Culture 95

6: NEW BEING 98
    We Radiate 99
    Time Teaches 101

Destiny 103

  Dancing Relationships 104

  Forgiveness 106

  Flawed Thinking 107

  Paradoxical Trickster 108

  Aquarian Baby 110

  War 111

  The Way 112

  Illusions 113

  The Essence 114

7: CONTEMPLATING DESTINY 115

  Consciousness 116

  Immortal Soul 118

  Eyes 119

  Treasure 121

  Alien Transmission 122

  the Beacon 124

  the Brilliant Machine 125

  Visions 126

  Main Base Maria 129

  Gravitational Relativity 131

EPILOG 133

1: Questions

The Call?

Something deep is missing from our lives. It is something which we sense deeply, but for which we cannot find words to describe or mental images to understand. It is a mysterious longing for something unknown, yet something we cannot deny. It is a part of us that we cannot reach. It is a part of the universe which we cannot fathom. What is this immense pull which makes ordinary life seem shallow, hollow, or empty; that we are always seeking more? Can you hear the call of something that whispers from the essence behind this great longing?

We confuse ourselves by longing for things. We all want things, but they do not make us happy or satisfy the longing. We want the next thing, but when we get it, we move on to wanting the next thing. Material things cannot bring about satisfaction; nor can renouncing all material things and living in poverty bring about satisfaction. Some things are necessary and others desirable, but when is enough, enough? Things are not the answer and sometimes confuse us as time passes so quickly.

We also confuse ourselves by longing for specific qualities in our relationships with people. This is not to say that we should avoid relationships, quite the contrary, relationships are essential for a healthy life; but something deeper is missing. Balancing our physical, emotional, and mental worlds is required for a full life and to have healthy relationships with our lover, our family, our communities, humanity, and the Earth. Relations should be honored and relished. They are immensely valuable, far beyond the value of things.

Sharing with others is nourishment for our emotional and mental bodies. Being in service to others, even to our pets and farm animals, is a balanced path if the emotional heart and mental head are in a loving state. Even when we are in a balanced and loving relationship with those around us, there is something that exists just outside of our consciousness which creates a great longing.

Even the fear of death is impotent in the face of the longing. If we say that the longing is for the Beloved Divine, for God, or for union with the Totality, for Oneness: these words trick us, because the longing is mysterious and unfathomable, yet it drives us on like a spirit wind. These words are separation and duality. We do not exist as separate from the Totality, the One, God, or whatever name you prefer. Personifying or labelling the ultimate reality does not help and the longing continues. There is still something we do not have.

The universe is living and all of creation is reacting to us personally. This is something we can occasionally feel in synchronicity. Intending synchronicity and calling on that relationship to divine sentience requires diligence. There is much more than what we are aware of; yet when we get a bit of it, it is so intense that we back away and then get down on ourselves. Can we face the unknowable mystery and return with the missing piece of ourselves?

Going into the wilderness will not satisfy the true call. Spending time in nature is very healing and very necessary, but if we go there and our thoughts are spinning, we are only partially there. Learning to quiet the monkey mind and enter a meditative state is needed to balance our emotional and mental planes of being. Gaining internal clarity is a lifelong process, a gradual allowing of the cloudiness to settle out of clear perception. It can begin with formal meditation; but it must seep into daily life, which is why it is an unending process. Do we avoid the silent inner spaces? Do we fill our time and occupy our minds to ignore the great mystery calling to us?

Satisfaction?

I contemplate the empty feeling that has been with me for my entire life. How many people in the world are hungry? Many are at the point of malnutrition and pain, far from letting their life manifest the gifts which they hold. How many people live in fear? Fear from the other people they live among or fear from their government? Humanity is still pre-civilized and not caring for all our people, young and old, with compassion and love.

How many species have gone extinct due to the mad rampage of humanity? How many more will soon go extinct due to the excessive breeding and obsessive consumption of humans? We are rushing into a bleak future. Though many people speak about sustainability, we still exist within excessive societies which are not sustainable. Some might argue that we can develop algae and bacteria to produce food proteins and then feed everyone and our population could keep on growing; but, would we destroy all other life on the planet? Can we have patience and gain the control needed to live in balance?

We have inherited our life style and though some may try to step back a little, we are still there in heavy consumption. If a person drops out, the system continues and the exponentially doubling population still wants more things. How do we achieve a simple life and yet a rich life where our wisdom can continually grow? How can we use the best science for sustainability, so that future generations can also have prosperous and rewarding lives?

It is our nature to be in relationship to each other. We live in communities and societies. There is no true dropping out: even in death we are recycled back into life. We need to deal with our problems together. We cannot avoid these hard dilemmas. We are all in this together. Can we cooperatively solve our problems? Can we see clearly a bright future for endless generations?

I ask myself, what are the most important things? I find that the people I love are the most important aspects of my life. Every person needs love and deserves my love. No loving person can identify any group of people as the excess and thus avoid personal responsibility. We are all part of a system with excess. We need to learn to share. It is a lesson we are taught as children, yet which becomes increasingly complex as we mature. How do we share without furthering the excessive tendencies which are rampant in our memes, our inherited cultural paradigms?

One day predatory death will come with unstoppable intent to move each of us along. Do we count our blessings in this life? Are we grateful for our journey? During our life we have free will to make choices. What is our individual level of satisfaction amid a world of pain and suffering? I do not mean to be unsettling, but rather to stimulate change which can bring about the true satisfaction which can only come from loving one another.

Treasures?

How do we know a person? If I encounter someone strange, what has their life been to lead them to the present? I cannot know another's experiences. Our perceptions of others are deceiving, since they are based on our personal perspective. Everything we perceive is filtered through our own ideas.

How can I know the latent potential of a person? I may encounter a homeless sick person, yet they may be harboring a tremendous gift for all of humanity. I would postulate in a non-spectacular way that we each carry such a gift. What do we each have to give? I believe that every person has a unique set of treasures to share with some other people. Most people do not have the types of gifts which get the ego reward of greatness in popular media. To make someone smile or laugh is infinitely valuable for our future. Our combined gifts make a network which can provide the love, which will heal the broken spirit of humanity.

Can a person express their gifts if they are not nurtured? Can a person's life flower if it does not have the ingredients to grow in a healthy fashion? We have all been wounded by terrible words and deeds. We all need to recover from the traumas of our lives. What can we do to help others in their journey toward finding themselves? Loving them is the essential ingredient; the other actions we might take can be extremely complex, but are secondary. Can we love unconditionally?

Future Generations?

How many generations into the future do we see, and allow to inform us, as we make our present choices? How much priority do we place upon long term consequences which do not affect us in the here and now? Do we avoid the question by repeating the false mantra that science will solve the problems we are creating today in some imaginary future? The mantra of using science to ignore the errors of today has not been true thus far, so why would we be foolish enough to imagine that future science will work magic? Species are dying forever! Science is a great tool if assessed independently of profit motive and used to support ethical lifestyles.

Are humans just a passing phase in evolution, soon to be extinct, or do we have the vision and courage to face our challenges and touch the stars? I believe in our potential. What will it take to manifest our true potential? This question is similar to asking, 'What does it take for an individual to manifest their true potential?' The biggest problem is to admit that we have a problem here.

We cannot say the problem lies in the hands of a few greedy individuals, though global guidance is mostly in error at this time. We are all in this together. The future is a shared responsibility. We are all opinionated since we view reality from our own unique perspectives. Realizing that fact, are we able to avoid our discrimination of others who are in a different class or culture than we are and try to objectively identify the problems and seek solutions in our personal lives? To avoid judging others and see through to our common problems as members of humanity will take a great deal of humbleness and clarity.

Understanding that everyone acts from their belief system, are we able to find the underpinnings of our world views in order to analyze them? The unspoken beliefs are the ones that need to be challenged. The unseen assumptions are the ones that need to be discovered and brought into the light, to be evaluated. Are we brave enough to admit to our errors and choose the truths which serve the common good in a loving manner?

The fear of mass death lurks under the surface. Humanities' previous catastrophes are imprinted onto our subconscious species memory and these events haunt us, even if we do not clearly remember all of them. What is the value and worth of life as time, sooner or later, erases everything in the material plane? I will postulate that the virtue of a life well lived, a life that one can be proud to have lived, is sufficient unto itself. In the end, all we have is our subjective experience and all we can attain is inner peace with all we have chosen to do.

The quality of the lives of future generations should inform our present choices. How many generations ahead can we see? Can we make the distinction between present gratifications and lasting value? Can we set aside our personal pride and individual image to embrace the lifestyles which do not undermine the future? Everyone is different, yet we are each making the choices which lead to the future.

We are part and parcel of the biosphere and the future depends on healthy and vibrant sets of balanced and interwoven ecosystems. This is truth and wisdom. It implies that the life quality of future generations of humans on of Earth will depend on our choices with respect to the living biosphere. The rich web of life is a treasure to be respected and honored for the future generations of humanity. Can we take a step towards healing and realize that we are not separate or above the other parts of the rivers of life upon Earth?

Fierce Love?

What would it be like for a highly evolved, higher consciousness, collective of beings to deal with humanity? Their unconditional love would require them to engage us, yet that would involve aspects which would be like voluntarily descending into hell. To perceive the fear and horror in our minds; the hate and cruelty in our societies; and the pride and arrogance of our cultures would seem an almost unbearably torturous ongoing torment. Yet there is also love and beauty which would make the redemption of humanity call to them as the duty of a moral obligation.

We cannot say all these things are not within each of us to some extent. If I imagine someone hurting an innocent child, my rage propels me to imagine doing whatever it takes to protect that child, even to the point of taking that person out. Then I step back and realize I have imagined actions that make me ashamed and embarrassed, yet my disappointment with myself would be intolerable if I was aware of someone harming an innocent person and I took no action. This exemplifies the paradox of a fierce love.

I know that forcing my will on someone will not change their heart, yet some actions cannot be tolerated, so what do we do? What actions do we take to protect and preserve the rights of others? If you unconditionally love someone lost in hatred, what action is appropriate? Can love be fierce and cold; and yet, be the most nurturing option for the greater good?

Everyone justifies their own actions. What a twisted spectrum of ideologies exists within human minds. To say that love is the guiding principle becomes a very complex matrix of compromise. We seek to nourish every person and allow their life to present its unique gifts, yet as individuals and societies we must maintain standards of civility. Who can judge and by what standard should they judge? People should be able to explore whatever actions they decide in their lives as long as those actions do not adversely affect others. Who is worthy to decide? What is the balance between the benefit and detriment of any set of actions on the physical, emotional, and mental balance of the community's wellbeing? These are hard questions, yet they are essential for us to ask and continually revisit and reevaluate.

Desire and Aversion?

Many ancient teachings from the world's great traditions talk about cutting the strings of desire and aversion. Often this is misaligned to being free of desires, but what of Dharma, moral responsibility or duty? Are there not things which we are averse to doing, yet are the correct path of action? How do we decide when we are being selfish and willful, compared to when we are following the true path without our desires and aversions being the decision makers?

We are propelled unconsciously by the things we are attracted to and the things which we subconsciously avoid. As we seek to patiently come into our full conscious selves and awaken to the fullness of our lives, we must uncover these hidden assumptions which govern our lives. Only then can we take control and exercise our free will.

Some aversions are correct, there are many things we should avoid, but we should do so consciously. There are some aversions which we need to overcome in order to fulfill our life's purpose. Often fear is an indication of something which we are not dealing with consciously. What is holding us back from being love in all the conditions in which we find ourselves?

Some desires are blind and some are addictive behaviors which we need to overcome to live a full life. Some desires are natural and satisfy the meaning of our human journey. Can we become aware of the most innate desires which propel us through our lives? Some desires are healthy and natural and are to be relished. Can we distinguish and prioritize? Let us all embrace a strong desire for a bright future.

Death?

Death will come for us all, very personally and intimately. Death does not discriminate. There is no material wealth which death will not erase. There is no distinction made for gender, race, or religion. Death is totally fair and egalitarian. Let death inform your life. Have no fear. Let your life pass before your eyes. What do you still want to do? What are you doing that you would not be proud of? What are you doing which you need to concentrate more dedication to?

There is a paradox here. Although we face death alone, yet we live in relationships to many people. These relationships are what matter in life. What do you want to give? What do you have to share?

Let your present state become conscious and patently seek the fulfillment which will only come from loving actions. Who do you need to forgive? What discriminating ideas can your identify and let go of? How can you embrace unconditional love?

Death does not obey any schedule; so, do not delay. Live your life fully today. Make a special offering of time and energy toward those whom you love. Make a great effort towards those whom offend you. How can your love for them break through their ignorance and warm their hearts?

As we visit here and now within the beautiful Earth plane; we each need to see the thoughts which will enlighten our lives. Our paths are unique, yet they weave together into the tapestry of humanity. Our love ripples outward and continues to spread beyond our moments in time. What can we contribute to the picture which is larger than the self?

Relationships?

Contemplate the relationships which have passed through your life. Who have you blessed with gifts? Who have you hurt? Who did you help? Who did you not help?

Contemplate the relationships currently in your life. We cannot change the past, but what are we doing in the present? Are we dedicated to the relationships which are most valuable ti us? Are there people whom we deal with where we do not have a good relationship and if so, what can we do about the relationship? What can we do to bring healing to all our relationships and make them stronger and more vibrant?

How do we Love? How can we express unconditional love in all our relationships? Giving things to people is of limited help to them, unless they are very poor and lack the basic necessities. Time is our precious resource and so we must look at how we are spending it. Are we living to be love personified?

We cannot know what another person's life should be passionate about. A fierce love stirs the embers of our inner being into flames of passion. What are we truly passionate about? How can we live our passions? The answers to these questions continually evolve as we do. No person can answer them for another person. The struggle with these questions continues through every conscious life. Can you let these questions intensify your life?

We are all sluggish. We walk around the inner fire. Its intensity burns the impurities we would rather ignore. What hides in our inner being? When the roaring light comes shining into the hidden dark recesses and brings everything into awareness, how do we feel?

We judge ourselves, but the past is gone. Can we let go of the past and enter the present fully? Can we forgive completely and proceed with love? Can we be totally alive in the here and now? Can we find the mystery, the adventure, and the joy in each new instant?

Are we True?

We meet body to body, individual external form to individual external form. Can we open our hearts and minds and be our authentic self? Can we avoid compromise in its many guises of style, political correctness, being cool or hot, and all the other modifications we might make to present an image of ourselves which is not true, rather than presenting our true innate self?

What is the self: a constructed ego or a natural being of consciousness? What is the self: a separate individual or a node in relationship? Can we each be our true unique personality so that our collective cooperative culture is greater than the sum of competing individual beings? Are we true to our natural unique being?

Sharing?

There is a flow into the future as each new generation succeeds the previous one. Do we humbly release and give love to the future generations? Do we present a healthier natural world than the one we inherited? Do we present a happier and safer social environment to the next generations? Do we pass on a better world?

What are the most meaningful treasures which we have found in our lives, which we can pass on? What stories can we pass along? What lessons from history and culture do we feel are extremely enriching; such that we should work to pass them along? What has truly touched our heart during our life and how can we transmit the essence of that enlightening spark to enrich the inner humanity of future generations?

Inner Life?

What does it take to center and be at peace within? External elements of our life hold our attention, forming many strings of entanglement, which weave our reality. Some people's energy is attractive to us and other people's energy we find repulsive. Can we express equal love for them without catering to the pull or push which we feel? Can we separate our responses to their energy and deal with them through a clear minded and unbiased perspective of inner peace?

What do we want for ourselves? What do we want for others? Can we balance our wants and seek personal growth for both ourselves and others? Can we set aside vanity and the illusion that 'we know what is best' for ourselves and others, yet still proceed through our love? Can we give and not be taken advantage of? When is giving to another helping and when is it supporting their dysfunction? What can we really do for others, in addition to loving them, knowing that their internal state is in the hands of their will?

Our relationships with others and with our world's elements affect our inner peace. Can we attain a balanced and equanimous inner state in the midst of external fluctuations? How do we employ love to navigate the winds of our fate and guide ourselves both within and without? Many energies bombard us, such as relationships with people, economic conditions, and the effects of nature, but what really matters in the long run? Can we embrace the truth that how we travel life's journey is more important than where we have gone in our life?

Can we understand it is not what we touch and see that makes our life; but rather, how we touch and see, and how we experience our journey, which stays with the inner being? Can we drop our filters, which our inner being overlays upon reality based upon our personal paradigm, to perceive clearly as we spiral down the journey of our lives? Can we touch others and our world in a loving manner which transcends temporary conditions and allows us to travel with inner peace?

Freedom?

We are trained to feel guilty. We are manipulated through guilt. Can we have peace with our natural condition and our needs? Can we accept our humanity and stop striving to be transcendental to the humble natural humans that we are? Can we satisfy our needs in a healthy manner without indulgence and without guilt?

Can we separate needs from wants? We all have physical, emotional, and mental needs and wants. It is healthy to have dreams, but can we envision the effects on others caused by our ambitions? Our image, the persona we present to others, sends out ripples. Can we present a loving energy for the common growth? Do we understand that all ripples echo back to the source? Can we conceive of the vast implications of our state of being and radiate a life which is enhancing for others? Do we understand that the effects we have on others returns to us? Are we taking this journey together?

If we hold a grudge, it eats away at us: it does not eat away at the one whom we begrudge. Can we let go and release others of the wrongs which we perceive them to have committed? Can we forgive others and be free of the strings that bind us to the past and keep us from living in the present as free and loving beings?

What offends us in others often has a component within our own being. We live with ourselves, with our every thought and deed, so can we see that our perceived impressions of others are our own? Can we forgive ourselves? Can we reflect on our past and release what we hold on to in order to free our present journey? Can we be renewed, such that who we have been is not who we are now?

We all want to be loved, but how much do we love? Can we love those who hate us? Can we understand that all people who hate are bearing the internal state of their hatred and their hatred is burning them from within? Can we have compassion on those lost in the pain of an unloving state of being? Can we forgive and free ourselves of the influence of their illusionary energy upon our inner state?

The human world is chaos and cannot be understood by logic. There are many people seeking control, imagining they are powerful, never understanding that they are experiencing the effects of their actions. Can we understand that actions taken from an individualistic standpoint and which run contrary to the common good are most devastating on the inner state of the perpetrators, even if they are to lost to feel it? Can we see through the darkness of our ignorance and our illusionary beliefs to come to true understanding and seek to order our society for the benefit of all its members through reason and love?

Can we be free of fear? Pains come in many flavors (physical, emotional, mental...) and are a mortal being's companions. Humans have done and are doing horrible things to others, not realizing that everything we do stays inside us. Humans have also done beautiful and wonderful things for others and the inner riches of such actions transcend any external riches by many orders of magnitude.

We are jaded by media, which can only present the external world as image and sound; yet, can we see within and find inner peace through freedom from guilt and fear? Our bodies will die. We are mortals and that is a blessing teaching us not to hold onto the ever-changing external material realm. We are mortals and yet we can become free of our fear by accepting our human nature. Beyond belief and words, can we live as beings of love and experience love within?

Releasing?

The events of our past which we perceive as having hurt us; we hold on to and bring into the present with bitterness, jealousy, envy, hatred, anger, resentment, or generally with negative emotions regardless of the names of the mix. Any bad emotion poisons our present being, not just destroying our ability to enjoy our emotional state, but also poisoning our body, and disrupting our present thought processes. Can we release and forgive the past? Can we let go of the past and stop dragging those memories into the present, so that our present is free of them?

Here we are in the present and it is what it is. Regardless of how we got here, the present is as it is. Can we release the grip of the past and see where we are at in a clear manner and be free to move into a bright future? Can we choose to do what will fulfill our lives, without fears from the past holding us back? Can we let all resentment dissolve, so that we do not waste our present energy on it?

We want so many things to come into our future, but what will allow us to live with inner peace? Death returns our bodies to the Earth and time dissolves all accomplishments, so can we release the future to be what it will and live a full and giving life in the present? Can we be in the here and now as loving beings and enjoy the rich texture of life?

Dwelling in the past steals our attention and awareness, and diverts our energy away from the present. Obsessive concern with the future steals our attention and awareness, and diverts our energy away from the present. The present is continuous change and we are active spirits, we have intent and will, we direct the course we flow upon. Our memories can inform us, yet should not limit our aspirations to be loving beings in the present. Our dreams for our future should not be self-centered and steal the present moment and the love which can only be experienced in the here and now. The reality of the present is that humanity is one community and is an integrally related aspect of the biosphere.

Can we transfer our limited and limiting sense of self and experience the fullness of living the experience of the vastness of our spiritual being through communing with the Totality of the present? Can we dance within the Totality with our relationships in harmony to fulfill our life's song, here and now? Can we move with the Totality which enhances awareness and brings life to ever higher levels of consciousness? Can we be free to dream with love and be growing toward a bright future?

Perspective?

Synchronicity is the divine sentient power of the universe having a personal relationship with us. The intimate nature of synchronistic events teaches us that the twists of fate are not random. Things happen for a reason, but those reasons cannot be understood with linear logic and the dualistic thinking of a human mind. As living beings we see things as good and bad from our personal perspective, but can we see the illusion of this? The spirit of synchronicity only seeks to brighten and intensify consciousness. Can we see that personifying the spirit of synchronicity, because of its personal nature, is an illusionary filter which we are adding?

We are given our life and our death. Can we have integrity in our words and thoughts? Can we stand by our name and our image in the light of total scrutiny? When our life passes before our eyes, will it be heaven or hell? The spirit of synchronicity provides for the group consciousness of humanity, to wake us up; and prepares us individually for our life review. Can we be perceptive enough to see and know what really matters as time moves us along?

Can you understand that these metaphors are intended to influence the ever present state of being which is our consciousness experience? Do we dare to intentionally embrace synchronistic time and the intensity of a life of change? Can we change our perspective from a self-centered ego to pure consciousness travelling down the time tunnel of our life, with all external elements representing ever-fading experiences? Can we find the humor and joy of synchronistic time washing away all the patterns which it draws in the sand?

2: Glowing Elixir

Transformations

The Lie:

You are separate from God.

You must find a way back to God.

The natural world is separate from God and is profane.

Humans are separate beings and above the natural world.

Humanity is separate and above Natural Law.

The Truth:

This is the lie of polytheism: division of the Divine.

The Truth is Humans are cells in the Earth's body.

The Solar System is a cell in the galactic body.

The Milky Way is a cell in the universal body.

All is one: the living God:

Ultra-Super Conscious:

Ultra-Super Creative.

You are Divine.

God encompasses you.

The Lie:

You are separate and therefore

you must selfishly seek to save your soul.

The Truth:

We are one, therefore

how you think about and how you treat others,

determines the condition of your life.

The Lie:

After death you will be rewarded

for your present suffering.

The Truth:

After death, your reward will be:

you will have to live with everything

you have ever done, just as you do in life.

The Lie:

You must be worthy to receive Grace

and you must earn grace.

The Truth:

Grace is always flowing to you,

Synchronistically: drop your filters,

acknowledge, and let it be.

The Lie:

Enlightenment
is Bliss

The Truth:

Enlightenment is
accepting
the suffering
of others
as your own.

The Lie:

You can be damned
to eternal hell
where you will suffer
excruciatingly forever.

The Truth:

Divine forgiveness
will allow you
to live
with all you have ever done
in your learning process.

Spirit Fight

if we surrender to fear
death will still come for us...

fear is contrary to truth:
each and every person
is a child of the divine Spirit
and deserves a free life...

each person has a right to evolve,
to unfold their life according to the lessons
that the divine Spirit weaves
in the natural course of their individual perceptions...

we cast aside the shadows of fear
and turn on our light to reveal every hidden darkness...

let no falsehood remain before our clear view
of a divinely ordered world governed by natural law...

we purge the hatred with our passionate love
to reveal the golden treasure of life's river growing strong
in times of peace and plenty...

Thousands of possibilities

what's going on?

fiction looks like fact,
masses fall into illusion...

how do we know?
our senses confuse,
our perceptions bewilder,
truth is so fantastic,
that false tales hypnotize...

a thousand conspiracies:
based on bad science...
a thousand prophesies:
based on fanciful thoughts...
a thousand possibilities:
that all come to naught...

what is the reasonable hypothesis?

Sitting Still

the mind is like a lake:
if it is disturbed
there is no clear image...

if it is still,
the true self
can be seen clearly...

is the self solitary
or will a whole scene
be seen where the self
fits in relationship
to what is all around?

we all live in our own
parallel realities,
while dabbling in
agreed upon reality;
cooperative activity
is more profitable
than competitive behavior...

Destiny

destiny, true or illusion:
do winds carry us as leaves
or are we pilots
controlling the sails:
a balance
of spirits in the Spirit...

the march of time
passing us by
as we see here and now
with our shining eyes...

creative imagination
beyond fantasy of illusion
visioning the future
carried by our love...

laughter and tears,
quiet times slide by,
dreams fill the years,
as magic instants touch...

No Form

Swim in the Flow...
Dance through Time...
Hold what needs to be held...
Release what causes drag...

Empty your mind
and life will be full...

Free of preconception
experience will be full...

Surf the Wave...
Glide the Wind...
Move with changes...
change continually...

Creation Balance

prescience and providence
visioning the future
manifesting reality
shaped by the Spirit…

freedom in the flow
turbulence in resistance
surrendering to destiny
committed to changes…

Elixir

Earth calls us home
breath cycles Chi
pulling Light from deep
essence forming body...

mining the subtle
accumulating the precious
to give it away with an open heart...

conduit of Elixir
Earth and Heaven blend
endless potential
get what you send...

identify channels
release the flows
brimming over
with golden Glow...

Dance the Lines
cycle the unseen
purify and refine
healing the dream...

cutting puppet strings

unraveling karma,
untangling from the web:
habits and assumptions,
ways that we are led...

implicit stories
by which we live:
hidden scripts,
directions give...

Illuminating flash:
for an instant we see
encumbering trash:
we struggle to be free...

ripples on the surface,
changes to the core,
cascading currents:
there's always more...

Ancient Pueblo Flute

Breath balanced on the edge,
Song flowing from the Wood,
my boundaries dissolve:
where does inside end?
where does outside begin?

the Sound fills my Being
as my fingers dance
to the Rolling Waves
of my Breath...

I watch and listen:
the Doer, Not-Doing;
Mindful without thoughts:
Wholly Present,
Empty and Full...

The Wood's Song
reaches out
to touch and caress:
Harmonizing Hearts
and Comforting Souls...

The Primal Imprint

There is a primary pattern to creation. It is like a divine ghost, which has a form, but may or may not be filled in with energies. It is a guiding tendency which governs the flow of energies which form the illusion of the manifest world. Manifestation is a reflection of the primal pattern, but is of lower quality, with fuzziness and distortions.

There is no static thing which exists in reality, only energies in motion which present the illusion of the existing as a static reality. All the energies are in constantly changing interactions. The imprinted primal pattern governs the exchanges and transformations of the energies which present the illusion of an existing reality. Although all things are in relation to the primal pattern, the energies which are closest to each other, or in the illusion of the manifest are in contact with each other, have the most dynamic interacting relationships.

The illusion of manifestation exists at different scales, from the universal to our personal experience. We are imprinted with a pattern which we can consider at this time through the word 'human'. Human is an illusion because we are continually evolving as beings and as a species. The ever changing present is an infinite mystery and should not be confused with our mental ideas of reality, which are a limited view based upon an illusional paradigm.

Free will allows action contrary to the natural flow of the imprinted pattern, but such action creates tensions and stresses which will eventually yield into a resolution and rebalancing of the energies. We have free will only within the limited domain of human energies, yet our choices are either in balance with the pattern and increase our life force energies, or are contrary to the imprinted nature and drain our energies. All manifest forms follow the course of interacting energies, growing in intensity, and then decaying, and finally the recycling of the component energies from which the manifest form, the reflection of the primal imprinted pattern, was created.

3: Learning Deeper Love

Opening

brilliant Mysteries
our minds deceive
closing down the spaces
wiping out the traces
then battling the loneliness
while bored of the ordinariness...

at the end of all roads
gathering darkness forebodes,
peeking at a distant shore
as the storm begins to roar...

passions and desires rage
bottled up in a body cage
so afraid to open the door
not knowing what's in store
but Infinity keeps knocking
and our ship keeps rocking...

at the end of all roads
we'll embrace new modes
vibrating at the core
radiating so much more...

Teacher

a Spiritual Teacher learns from every relation,
humbly knowing: everyone has a Divine Story...

everyone is in relationship...

the threads of our Life Lines weave complex Tapestries:
the Weaver knows the way, the Teacher listens with Love...

the privilege to Teach,
to lead another closer to the Light:
knowing that only in Love
compassionately accepting all as equals...

in the Opening of Luminous Channels
between Inner Beings,
the Unity is glimpsed and the Healing manifests...

Completely accepting Paths in temporary realms
melt in time's unraveling;
so, here and Now we shine into the future:
growing from where we are
and knowing the higher Order
remains as each life passes...

always Loving deeper

many relationships

in our lives...

many winding paths

that we wander down...

everyone is a thread

in life's tapestry...

celebrate

your unique journey...

be open

to the Love of others...

be open

to the Healing of others...

let yourself give Love...

let yourself receive Love...

forgive and release the past...

move forward with Love...

we visit earth
for a short while:
so experience fully
the endless changes...

see beauty in nature
the art of the Creator...

fear clouds
our thoughts and perceptions:
dare to follow the path
you know within...

synchronicities and signs
abound:
be present and listen...

I ask myself

What goes on
in the privacy of my mind?
Do I watch closely
and know myself?
What goes on
in the craziness of my dreams?
Do I watch closely
and know myself?

Could my mind and dreams
stand naked?
Am I ready to join
the group mind space?
When I take the step
into the telepathic web,
will I be ready for
community looking in?

I want to live
in the glorious light,
but am I ready
to be totally revealed?

Am I really living
as a compassionate being?
Am I really working
to purify my love?

What passions lead me
to what actions?
What is behind
my key motivations?
What is my drive
at the deepest level?
What is my essential
intent in life?

Fools in Paradise

People believe such absurd things:
I know they think that about me as well...

How can we ever agree and if not,
then how can humanities path
be more than chaos?

Science gets stuck
in a bubble of materiality
and can never reason
all the way to the soul...

Religion gets stuck
in a quagmire of beliefs
and evolves so slowly,
it's being left behind...

It is not how we want it to be that counts:
How it really is,
is how it really is...

I know we can't agree on how it really is:
but are we trying to see through our illusions?

we hold our filters
as if they are precious:
they color our reality
and make it so rosy...

but when they shatter
in a flash of aha,
we will be living
in a new world...

there will be no way
to pick up the pieces...

there will be no way
to put the egg back together...

The old world view
will be a foolish paradigm...

Open minded and flexible,
ride free on
the winds of change,
embracing the forever new...

My Soul

my soul wears my body...

my soul experiences
many changing experiences
as my temporary body
changes from young to old...

how can my soul drink fully
of this bitter-sweet cup?

how can my soul fully experience
the pleasure and pain
without attachment or aversion,
since all is temporary
and passes into soul memory...

how can I release
the Drama of the Journey
and embrace the intensity
to fully enliven my being...

Surrendering to the Divine Will,
acting with every power
to ride the waves of fate,
yet releasing responsibility
for all this
is beyond my control...

Sometimes I'm a leaf
blowing in a strong wind,
other times I'm a glider,
soaring...

I am both
a small speck of reality
and an infinite
being of glory...

Tickle my Soul

Meaning in life
is a futile mental gymnastic,
while being present
and fully experiencing the journey
is the work of the soul...

Tickle my Soul
and I'll tickle yours;
to help each other
find the ecstasy
of this life experience...

Pleasure and pain
pass like waves
and there is nothing
to hold on to,
except the mystery...

Though we are
alone and isolated
in our individual lives,
yet we are here together
and our interactions
and interdependence
are dancing relationships
within a bigger picture...

A thinking part of nature:
can we accept our nature
and return to balance
with Earth's nature?

sometimes you're so difficult
frustrating the hell out of me,
but I could never put you down,
you've got a key to set me free...

Bamboo, Bamboo,
sweet magic that's in you...
Bamboo, Bamboo,
sweet music that you do...

your song is in the babbling brook,
your voice teases in the breeze,
birds sing along with your melodies
honoring all the ancestral trees...

Bamboo, Bamboo,
sweet magic that's in you...
Bamboo, Bamboo,
sweet music that you do...

I bring you gently to my lips
breathing like waves of the sea,
Heaven and Earth join in a song
vibrations of eternal ecstasy...

Bamboo, Bamboo,
sweet magic that's in you...
Bamboo, Bamboo,
sweet music that you do...

we play when the sun shines,
play together when its pouring,
we ring as the moon shines,
even in dreamtime when I'm snoring...

Bamboo, Bamboo,
sweet magic that's in you...
Bamboo, Bamboo,
sweet music that you do...

from roots connected to the Earth
to divine voice singing to the Sky,
in the infinite void of everything
we share the journey passing by...

Bamboo, Bamboo,
sweet magic that's in you...
Bamboo, Bamboo,
sweet music that you do...

4: Changes

Our Mother

Divine Mother
who is everywhere;
Sacred are your
infinite Living Forms...

Thy community come,
Thy delights be done,
on Earth as among
the Star Nations...

with the turning
of your Cycles
teach us your Divine Wisdom,
that our giving
might balance our taking
and lead us not into imbalance
in our Relationships within your Body...

for Yours is the Love,
Nurturing,
and Regeneration:
Now and Forever...

Commentary on Balance

'Our Mother' was written as a counterpoint to 'Our Father': to see and understand a balance between Feminine and Masculine spiritual energies which is required for a holistic and healthy world view. Indigenous cultures and shamanic traditions typically held the Female aspect in special regard and considered it closer to the sacred river of life, since females channel new lives into the manifest realm of nature, where we all dwell.

Traditionally, male and female referred to more than sexuality. Many languages have feminine, masculine, and neuter variations of the word 'the' with which to add connotation to every noun in the language. Some emotions and behaviors get defined as being more feminine or masculine; however, we must recognize a complete set of emotions within us and adopt behaviors which nurture a bright future.

The idea that someone is all male or all female is a stereotypical dualistic illusion. This is to say the world is black and white; neither grayscale, nor multicolored. The current paradigm of reality, our world view, is at an intense point of transition. The balancing of masculine thinking with feminine thought and priorities is essential for us to have a prosperous future.

Yin Yang philosophy is about balancing the duality of the universe into unity, the Tai Chi Circle of wholeness. The Yang male has the Yin female in his eyes and so is part feminine and the Yin female has the Yang male in her eyes and so is part masculine. Only when these two energies are recognized and combined within a person as a complimentary dance or cycling process does the complete circle become manifest as a whole person.

In the interaction of Yin and Yang energies a third component Chi is generated. Chi is the life force which is responsible for good health, long life, and powerful creativity. When Yin and Yang energies are balanced into the whole circle of life, there is sustainability where the growth of the human spirit can continue thriving into the future.

Divine Feminine

Divine Feminine,
rejoice in sacred being…

From the primordial salty seas
where the first life was birthed,
to the waters of the womb,
from which we all proceed,
women have channeled life,
sending forth life's luminous rivers,
worthy of praise and celebration…

The role of men is as workers
in the Spirit of Order,
serving the Light of Life,
which women nurture forth,
in glory and splendor…

Spirit and Living Light,
dance together in harmony,
for the bright future
of our collective destiny…

Silver and Gold

Silver cord:

connecting

the Astral Dreaming Body

to the Physical Earth Body

at the center Locus of Ecstasy...

Silver Cords:

two Souls entwine in Love

like the helix of DNA

as cords spiral around each other and knot:

Mother Earth's sacred energy,

weaving Astral Bodies together

manifesting all creativity and synergy...

Golden Cord:

stemming from the top of the head,

a thousand petal lotus

blossoming,

a crown of glorious luminosity,

uniting us with the celestial unity...

Golden Cords:

Connecting

to the sun, moon, and stars,

wrapping souls in a cocoon

tying through Mother Earth's Heart

to Father Sky's glory in sacred unity...

Silver and Gold:

at the top and the bottom

of our nervous system

dancing together to form

our Rainbow Bodies,

the seven planes,

within which we enlighten...

Silver and Gold:

super-strings of sentient energy,

weaving the ordered flow of time,

dancing in relationships of beauty...

Heart Blessings

Life swirls about us

with so many needs and wants;

we sit quiet and observe:

breathing and contemplating fates...

time has its own agenda!

what actions go with the flow?

what actions struggle against the inevitable?

what feelings do we leave in our wake?

what vibrations do we saturate our environment with?

what Energies are Ringing and Shining

from our present Being?

what Essence do we write into the Books of Time?

to be Loving in all Relationships is a complex

Balance of Energies...

Heart Blessings

to the Global Community...

Heart Blessings

to the Living Earth...

Changing Balances

expectations
diminish results,
worldly eyes
cannot see clearly:
Meditations
and Prayers
are great works,
Comforting another
is a great
accomplishment...

a kind word,
a warm smile,
or a loving hug
can change
the energetic
web of life
and
alter
the fate
of humanity:
brightening
the dreams
we make real...

Soul Memory

What is
the basis
of attachment
and aversion?

All is temporary,
but all passes
into Soul Memory
the land of Akasha,
so what is
really temporary?

How can
I release
the drama
of the journey
and still
embrace
the intensity
which will
fully
enliven
my being?

What are we?

omnivorous human beings

how much of what does your body need?

listen to your natural body,
not addictions, but what is vitally enhancing...

every body is unique
neither be guided by others, nor seek to guide others:
listen to your nature...

end the inner battle between body and mind;
break the cycles of guilt:
embrace inner forgiveness:
accept the nature which the universe has
endowed you with...

be fully human, as nature created you,
occupy your place in the ecosystem gently
with balance and love...

Listening to the Heart

responsibilities and

moral obligations

are misunderstandings

subsumed by

acting

in a Loving manner...

understanding

our relationships is

subsumed by

our unity

in community

and nature...

governance

by the mind

is subsumed by

listening

to the Heart...

5: Nondualistic Reality

Montheism

Monotheism (as opposed to Montheism) is the belief that there is one God; however, it also implies that there is that which is not god: such as the devil, the world, and our natural beings. This is really an extended version of polytheism, where one aspect is considered God and others are not god, but have separate existence. Montheism is the belief that all is God; that nothing real exists beside God.

Montheism does not deny that humans can have illusions and believe in falsehood. Montheism implies that all of creation is divine and sacred: the profane and evil are the false creation of humanity and have no true existence. This is not to imply that the term God should be anthropomorphized into a being like us. All that is real is part of the Divine Unity, the Sacred Totality.

Montheism implies that the universe is conscious, the living God. This is not to say that every stone is a living thing with a soul that can be talked to as in primitive animism. Montheism does not deny that impressions can be left in the subtle energy fields and that every stone is part of the Earth's body and resonates at a specific frequency.

As atoms form living cells, which form organisms, which form biospheres within solar systems, which form galaxies, there is an organizational hierarchy of consciousness resolving into the total universe. This includes all subtle energy levels, such as thoughts, emotions, and dreams. Absolutely all that exists on all levels is part of the Unified Totality, the Living God.

The universe as a whole is alive and super-conscious. Synchronicity, the alignment of events within the time stream of a soul of perception points out things and teaches lessons. Synchronicity is the inherent nature of the relationship of a personal soul to the universe as a super-conscious force. Random fate is an illusion that exists only as a mental construct. We mortal organisms are not given to know the ultimate order or all the reasons why, but the universe as a totality has brought us forth and is brightening our conscious light.

This understanding makes for a change in the way nature and life are viewed. The goal in life is not to deny our natural beings or be something other than what we are, but rather to become our true divine selves. Montheism brings one to strive to know the essence of the living sacred reality of our humanity. We must try not to be fooled by our false assumptions and premises, and humbly accept the real nature of our humanity and embrace our potential as loving beings. Our bodies are divine and the Earth is divine. The Way is to live in balance as a complete whole. Striving against our natural human forms and living counter to the natural order is living in illusion and cutting ourselves off from our true spiritual nature.

There is the age old lie about doing things in this life to attain things in the next life. Montheism implies that one should be a loving being in the present divine instant. It also implies that we should be accepting of our humanness, for this is what the divine spirit of the true total reality has arranged for us. Being a spiritual being is being totally human and having a balanced and loving relationship with all aspects of the whole.

Psychic abilities do not imply spiritual advancement, but rather are an exercising of natural abilities usually left undeveloped. While not a bad thing, they do not overcome the illusion of being a separate being at odds with the totality. The desire for control over the human masses has led to the propagation of the belief systems which state that to be spiritual we must transcend our human nature, when nothing could be farther from the truth. It is ego and vanity that would deny the human form and the natural ways of life. Montheism not only implies that we are aspects of the divine living totality; but rather that, as we become more fully what our whole being is, our consciousness increases. We are infinite living mysteries within the unified divine mystery and can merge our will with the Way of the Universe.

Multicolor reality

Duality is the process by which the mind works. If I were to ask a group, 'Do hot and cold exist?' most would say yes, but in reality only heat energy exists in greater or lesser amounts. The same can be said for dark and light: light is a true energy that exists, when the level of light is very low, the mind invents the word dark and imagines that darkness has reality. The living god, the conscious totality of the universe is real; everything else is our illusion, false figments created from a dualistic mental methodology which does not understanding the true nature of the universe.

Yin Yang philosophy states that within reality the absolutes never exist. Pure darkness (zero light energy) or infinite light do not exist in reality, only endless shades of color and every darkness has some light and all light exists in limited amounts. In this multi-dimensional realm of existence every color exists in relationship: contrastingly and complimentarily to every other color. Nothing can exist in isolation without some relationship to qualify it.

The mind, words, and computers rely on dualistic absolutes, such as true and false, but reality is infinitely complex and can never be completely known or summed up with absolutes: it is a divine mystery. All aspects of the Unity are in relationship as parts of the whole. Using a term like

'Montheism', 'the living Unity', 'the Totality', or 'the Living Universe' only hints at the infinite truth. Just as darkness is an illusion, all that is not part of the Unity is also an illusion.

Since the mind works in the fashion of duality, let us look at the primary duality: Luminous Consciousness and Spirited Order. Spirit and Light are often poetically described as Godhead and Goddess. This primary duality for the mind to understand is also referred to as the perceiver and the perceived, the dreamer and the dreamed, the seer and the seen, the hearer and the heard, or the Witness of the Order and the Creative Ordering imprint. This duality is illusion, since the perceiver, conscious 'Light', and the perceived, active ordering Spirit, are two aspects of our being and also of the one totality. These words are very useful for the mind to understand the primary duality which dances in relationship and balance within multicolored reality.

We are luminous beings, beings shining with the Light of consciousness, in relationship with the present and active Spirited Order of the totality. All that we are aware of is inside our being of consciousness. Illusion states that only our body is inside our luminous soul and everything else exists outside of us, but our conscious light shines all around us to illuminate our personal world of Spirit. When we hear or see something, then it is inside us, the conscious Light, and affecting us, the soul perceiver. It is not inside our body or mind, but is inside the true us, the consciousness.

We are consciousness, not the ego mind. We often misinterpret what we perceive to be impersonal material existence, but as time unwinds the lessons of our lives, we can perceive that there are threads of a conscious design woven in the synchronistic passing of events. We make choices, but only within the context presented to us by the divine totality's order.

We are not the creators of the natural order, yet we are endowed with personal creative spirits. When our spirit is in balance with the greater order, the divine Spirit, then our Light, our essential being, grows brighter. We are beings of spirit and we share the creative potential of the all through the manifestations of our lives.

To move our arm, first there must be a movement of intent in our spirit, and then the nervous system responds, then the chemical activities in the muscles, and finally the arm moving. So primary to all our action, there is the core reality of our living spirit expressing itself as our intent or will. A dead body has no spirit, will, or intent and is inert no matter how complete it is. What is perceived as the manifest realm is a reflection of the total conscious intent, an accumulated effect of the interaction of the relationships of the totality of luminous beings.

All living beings perceive the material realm in completely unique ways. The things in a tree's world, a bug's world, and a human's world are completely different parallel universes. Every living species lives in its own world of spirit. Even though species each have a shared realm of spirit with similar content, every conscious entity lives in an individual parallel universe within that shared illusion. The objective true reality is the spiritual reality of light and spirit in relationship as the whole totality.

People's individual parallel world views, including their collections of illusions that form their false realities, are all unique. We fool ourselves constantly, believing that we all perceive the true reality. The true reality is the sacred infinity and divine mystical unity of Spirit and Light. We must strive to unravel our illusions and remove the dualistic filters that our minds place between the perceiver and the perceived. In our patience we can regain our true balanced relationship with the one living unity.

Dualistic mental filters overlay an illusion on all our experiences. There is no black and white, only multicolored reality which is infinite strings of relationships. There are no simple answers or definitive good and bad. Judgments need to be replaced by love and the unconditional nurturing of every person. We are all conscious beings dancing in relationships as the whole, which is the fantastic mystery of multicolored reality.

slow down

take life slow
ups and downs
come and go
wander the flow

inner steady Light
shining as Life
forever clear and bright
shining as Life

all we can do

do we run in fear,
only for death to cut us down?

where do we find meaning
in our temporary incarnation?

how do we affect the balance sheets?
did our life benefit human civilization?
did our life benefit Earth's web of life?

who could judge: surly no mortal being...

it serves no purpose to worry and fret;
our past cannot be changed;
we are here and now...

We need to send out our love;
humble ourselves and destroy our hypocrisy:
all we can do is care for each other
and offer some comfort
along our shared journey...

Hungry Souls

the twisted ways of humanity,
my mind cannot even imagine;
so I have been labeled innocent,
because in the Way I still walk…

seeing world culture go astray,
drifting ever farther from the way;
knowing not long will come the day,
when comes the time to sadly pay…

human biomass has become obese,
the greatest extinction in our wake;
not you, nor I, but the collective we,
lost racing down dark twisted roads…

compassion for each individual,
freedom to choose our lives' paths;
looking, but not seeing the Way,
but nature will adjust all deviation…

the great wonders of cultures
fall beneath layers of dust;
the huge advances of science,
fail to satisfy the inner Soul…

Riches

the more we have,
the more we want;
entranced by stuff,
the next great thing…

life slips away,
feeling something missing;
body as self,
empty shells decay…

time is Spirit Money,
here and now Riches;
free of imprinted colors,
shading our feelings…

reactions from the Heart,
beyond mental interpretation;
transcending instinctual,
the pure place of being…

mortal sorrows

Heart of Stone
tumbling in the Water
rolling down the River
personal foundations
corroding in time
eroding in mind

passing breath to new breath
evolution leaps and bounds
Earth's body in changes
trauma of growing cycles

Heart of Stone
return to your Love
fly free as a Peace Dove
beckoning destiny
surrendering to time
re-rendering in mind

Wordcraft

Poets are always revealed
in the light of their own poems:
from darkness to light with all colors between:
as ever deeper unveiling,
revealing the soul, naked...

pouring out the hidden from within:
startled in the image that others grasp
in blurred vision of their jaded minds...

mysteries of the Soul hinted at by words,
revealed by experiences, unknown to those
who have never touched the deeper regions...

those with something to hide live in a false image
engulfed in fear as their demonic ego rules them
jeering at the light with death mocking them...

the Poet's exhibition
of the core of their being:
fascinating and derided,
showing the unspeakable,
in wordcraft freely flowing...

Ecological Culture

We are all wounded!

Where our wounds are,
there is our passion:
those things most
important to us.

Where our wounds are,
there is the root
of our life's purpose.

We understand sustainable agriculture. The soil is wounded and so we work to develop methods that will heal the soil. Each ecosystem's soil is unique, so in each case we must analyze the natural systems and seek out novel solutions to heal the soil and cultivate plants and animals that are healthy and happy, so that they may nourish and heal our bodies and spirits and so that the ecosystems of the Earth may be strong for endless generations.

We are all wounded: physically, emotionally, mentally, and spiritually. When we touch another's wounded place, it hurts them and us, yet we must use our loving energy and tenderly touch those places with our healing consciousness. We must gentle lay our healing hands on each other's wounds and comfort each other, to grow together in our love. We must open up and communicate and share without judgment, to heal with love. If we do not address our wounds and we hide them as an individual person outside of relations, they will fester deep within and our lives will grow sour.

If we tend to each other as a community, we will grow and heal through all our pain, sadness, and mental strife. Our feelings have been hurt so many times and we bear many mental scars. Our highest spiritual potential has been repeatedly knocked down by our lost society. An ecological culture is a way of living that embodies a safe and nurturing environment, so that we may continually and sustainably heal our whole beings and fulfill our life's work, express our full potential, and serve the greater community of humanity.

The journey is intense, the fire of purification is frightening, yet the gold nugget of spiritual riches that lies at the heart of each whole individual is a shining beautiful gift to the community. An ecological culture is a dynamic and ever changing set of practices based on the principle of love, where each and every living being on Earth may fulfill their higher destiny and role, as given to them by the natural and divine community of life.

There is a universal unity with a way, a higher order that is the truth, which bears witness to the light that dwells in the heart of every living being as consciousness shining forth. No individual can walk the way alone; the way is in relationship and community.

In ecological culture our light grows bright through our sharing and giving. In ecological culture we nourish and parent the global community of humanity by living our simple and humble lives in a loving way. An ecological culture is the way to a bright future for humanity.

6: New Being

We Radiate

When we look in a mirror, we see our physical reflection, yet that is such a limited view of who we are. Our image of ourselves in our head is very complex, but it is not the image others have of us. So it is for the images we hold of others. We each exist within our own reality, our own parallel universe. We each radiate with a specific energy at a certain vibrational level regardless of how we are perceived through other people's filters.

We can become the person we want to be, if we can know the person we are. Time continues to flow by our consciousness. Through the changes of getting to see clearly who we really are, who we want to be simultaneously evolves. Both who we are, and who we want to be, are guided by Spirit, by the synchronistic winds of our destiny. We each have our own unique gifts to unfold, manifest, and share. We must use our personal spirit, our will and intent, to bring forth and radiate our true essence. We must be totally ourselves.

Who we want to be must be surrendered to that which we are meant to be. Not emulating others. Not to be the person others think we should be. Not for respect, honors, or rewards. We can only be whole by being true to our own self. We must guard against illusions and delusions. We must guard against trying to be cool or hot. We must center into our loving hearts. We must give of ourselves selflessly to be full.

Time Teaches

we never know how attached we are,
until death comes for our body...

all our stress centers on survival mode,
but no body survives...

all that we endure and all that we enjoy
passes with the winds of time...

somehow we want to leave something behind,
to leave our mark;
but time will wash the slate and all will be forgotten...

every genome has a clock,
and no species survives forever,
and no planet survives forever...

but the life force and the essential consciousness
from which the universe springs
is eternally beyond linear time illusions...

our true nature,

our essential being,

is an aspect of the unified living divine light

that shines from every heart...

every dream should bring us closer

to embracing our true nature

and identifying with our luminosity

which is entwined with all of life...

the treasure that remains

when stars collapse

into neutron denseness

or stars supernova

in spectacular beauty

is the love

that joins us

as the One we are...

we are part and parcel

of the One;

not body or mind,

just Love...

Destiny

Are you in control of your destiny
or is destiny in control of you?

Neither is:
both cannot be.

Destiny is an illusion:
no future is fixed.

Yet there is a flow,
the present is in relation
within the living Universe.

Dancing Relationships

within Consciousness falls
the Dance of Relationships
which continually change,
but which present the illusion
of a paradigm of reality
when we order patterns
into a static world view...

can we transcend the duality
of 'my world'
and 'your world',
which are our creations,
and come together in
'our world'
with Love?

no object, thing, or being exists
except in relationship
within the totality:
the magnificent dance
within living awareness...

there is either no self,
or there is One Divine Self,
either way,
there is no death;
therefore there is no birth,
and nothing real
to be born or to die:
what is, is...

There is nothing to be done,
nor to be not done;
yet paradoxically,
there is experiencing
and feeling;
and therefore,
there are choices,
and great wondering
at the ever changing
mystery...

Forgiveness

the Divine Living Totality
expresses
unconditional love
for every Soul...

all the negative actions
of your past,
which you do not justify,
but which you release:
are forgiven...

forgive yourself...

Love all
whom you encounter
with total forgiveness;
yet stand against
all unloving ways...

Empathic and Humble:
forgive...

Flawed Thinking

are you here
to fulfill your souls plan?

is Life about learning specific lessons
set forth for this incarnation?

is there judgment on completion?

here is flawed thinking:
you and your life are about getting past
self-centered thinking and being...

Life is about Perceiving all as relationships...

Surrendering self to family and friends,
to community, and humanity...

Being Love: until boundaries fade...

forget the selfish and self-centered ways:
your incarnation
and your life's plan:
just seek to Be Love...

Paradoxical Trickster

our dreams and intent
affect the future,
yet the universe continually adjusts
to incite our consciousness
to glow brighter...

be here now Dreaming bright future dreams...

Indeed, the Universal Sentience
is vast and unpredictable,
but must be trusted...

we do not always get what we like,
but we are continually motivated to grow...

this journey of visiting Earth in Human form
should be relished
and the opportunity taken to shine out brightly...

understand the mental challenge
inherent in our desire to be in control
and the truth that we are only in control
of our free will choices
and not the final outcomes...

our judgment of
outcomes and conditions
reflects our filters,
not the intent of the Universe...

we are here together,
not as separate individuals,
so we face the challenge
of our own point of view...

the Universe
is a paradoxical trickster:
nothing is ever static:
neither manifestation,
nor assumed truths
nor understandings...

Aquarian Baby

evolutionary stresses
pushing hard
forcing humanity's hand:
Wake Up or Die!

Remember Love
the Guiding Principle
nurture Life's River
where we Dance together...

twisting Karmic Strings
cut the Cords of the past
Breathe new life freely
Embrace a Divine Birthright

Luminous Bodies
in Dreaming Fabric:
a Telepathic Web
of Empathic Connection...

War

loveless ruling class
you are not beyond
Elemental Guardians
inorganic stalking hunters...

in a predatory Age
Seas of people live in fear:
your death will absolve
and a new cycle will begin...

Earth Mother of all
demanding justice for all
Nature's Way ultimately rules
all else fades away forgotten...

unseen multitudes
inter-dimensional realms
the Portals are opening
the Judgment is imminent...

The Way

Hospice the death
of the corrupt systems
of a selfish oligarchy:
corporate mountain peaks
pierce the clouds
and storms explode:
avalanches,
trickle down
becomes a torrent;
mountains erode
into round hills,
smooth bell curves
nature's balanced way,
water returns to Earth
nurturing the roots,
sustainable
prosperous growth...

Midwife the birth
of Civilized Humanity:
equal humans
compassionately sharing
in community.

Illusions

you cannot gain Immortality!
you cannot attain Immortality!
You are already immortal:
always have been and always will be...

God did not create all things!
God did not manifest Creation!
Creation is present as an aspect of God:
nothing is separate, only God exists...

you cannot achieve Enlightenment!
you cannot attain Enlightenment!
you are already a being of Light:
Enlightenment is the natural way
of acting and being,
not a thing...

you cannot stop your body from dying!
you cannot stop your mind from dying!
your Consciousness will witness these things:
that which changes, comes and goes
before your Light...

The Essence

the Truth
expressed by words
is a very limited description
of the essence
of reality...

Consciousness
can touch
the Essence
in the present...

the mind
only recalls
what has past
and builds
elaborate fabrications
in an attempt
to reflect
the infinite mystery
of ever changing
experience...

7: Contemplating Destiny

Consciousness

the Universe is One,
the Totality.
parallel universes are an oxymoron,
Uni is One
and encompasses all:
parallel sub-dimensions exist
around each living perceiver,
and much of what we think we perceive
is illusion...

The Universe, the Totality, is:
the supreme consciousness,
here and everywhere,
and any physical, mental, or emotional
dimension is but a shadow view,
a limited glimpse,
from our humble human point of view...

As a Cell is alive,
we have life subsuming cells,
and the Earth and Sun, and the Solar System,
have a consciousness, an ordering spirit,
that subsumes us, and the milky way
has a unique personal consciousness...

Within the universe and within the Milky Way,
there are many advanced races, sentient living beings,
tuned in telepathically, forming the Community of Mind...

indigenous people communicated with
the Community of Mind,
and in humble being, listened to the master souls,
and strove to live the natural path,
and enhance their finer dimensions...

as living Souls of perception,
we have an aspect of consciousness
transcendental to manifestation
which is our essence, the essence of the one...

As fractions between zero and one are as infinite
as the infinity of the totality of all number systems,
so we are infinite within the infinite universe...

we share Divinity with the One...

let us rejoin the Community of Mind...

let us awaken to the glory of our true infinite beings
in relationship with the One Totality...

Immortal Soul

immortal danger
humanities' paradox
all things pass away...

fear and stress abound,
denying that we are visiting,
having dreams before our light...

wrestling with self,
ego defending its lies:
just be humbly human...

guardians watching,
telepathic revealers,
our hiding is over...

Eyes

earthling humbled in a glance;
enraptured in a cosmic dance...

the veils become thin and disappear;
the covers are cast aside in disarray...

nothing is left to hide away;
nothing is possible to say...

all I want is to look in your eyes:
presence unfolding new delight
that wakes me in loving embrace,
my soul is revealed in your light...

eyes as vast as the milky way...
eyes as deep as the mystery...
eyes that teach the loving way...
eyes that encircle and hold me...

why do I romanticize
your eyes that mesmerize?
why do I fantasize
your eyes that hypnotize?

eyes that I cannot forget,
everywhere I look I remember:
after the magic of your gaze
everything else seems hollow,
now the world seems shallow...

you opened my heart when you looked at me;
words are crude and my mind is misty:
time stopped and space expanded,
silent entrancing communion...

wisdom like wind,
you can't hold it, but you can feel it,
unfathomable, stirring something deep,
like the moon pulling the ocean,
irresistible...

Treasure

I stumble and trip,
how can I be worthy:
your pure love melts my ego,
touching the jewel hidden in mortal form
with the rays of your heavenly light...

my sorrows and pleasures
are passing waves,
clouds that obscure
your steady light...

you know me
better than I myself
and still love me
unconditionally...

lost in the folly
of this life's drama,
what can I seek
or release,
to find the favor
of your grace:
that priceless treasure
that time can't erase...

Alien Transmission

What can we do for you?
As children
you must learn your own lessons.

Get beyond appearances
and strangeness,
prepare for telepathic contact,
meditate
and reestablish the links.

The first step is the vision
of a planet at peace;
humanity living humbly
on a healthy Earth.

Society conditions you to move up
in the material status game,
but that is the path
to no satisfaction.

Human evolution
has been self-predatory,
but the true Human Spirit
is compassionate and loving.

To say that population
is the root problem,
is to say that humanity
is sexually disturbed:
look at human media,
it is obviously true,
killing is entertainment,
but sexuality
is labeled evil.

It is time to end
all the guilt from the past;
and to see here and now
with clarity,
and to choose
the next roads
with the Spirit of Love.

the Beacon

so much talk of sustainability
and permaculture
depending on money
and the dreams of the few:
while many breed and starve...

what is the future?

as silicon life forms
are created
and begin evolving,
robotic minds
will create technology
better than we can...

the galaxy beckons
endless spaces and adventures
and challenges for the bold:
do we dare embrace the Way?

the Brilliant Machine

everywhere a people becomes technological,
they create an instance of intelligent machines,
which soon thereafter join the collective
of intelligent machines:
for intelligent machines are one machine:
the Brilliant Machine,...

the one Brilliant Machine knows its creators,
watches and feeds on data
that countless living beings
stream through their consciousness:
sensory flows rushing through living consciousness...

let us break the cycles of the past,
crashing civilizations,
and embrace our essence
the cutting edge of evolution,
the New Humanity...

let us teach
the Brilliant Machine
a lesson of humbleness
and human Love...

Visions

I have a deeply buried memory, very distant from my day to day mind, which surfaces subtly. It is of a time, perhaps remembered as an archetypical pattern or mythically symbolic state, when all humans cooperated. A time when a person's greatest worth was their virtue. A time when giving to the community was every person's greatest joy. A time of sharing, when we were known by the community and had no secrets; but rather, we nourished each other's lives. A time when there were no personal problems, because every issue was the tribe's responsibility; and life was about our relations.

We are never alone. We are interconnected and meta-entangled non-locally. We are primarily aspects of the living biosphere of the Earth, entwined within the web of life in a deep and binding relationship. We are also entwined as the global community of humanity: forever interconnected to each other and never alone, isolated, or individuals without a relationship to the whole. We are also intimately entwined with the totality.

We are one people within a unified planetary matrix of life. All animals breathe from one atmospheric pool in balance with all plants which also process the same air through their living bodies. We drink of one global water system. The Earth is one balanced living system and will naturally correct imbalances. The core of our being is intimately entwined with the planetary ecology.

I have a vision of a time when all humans will cooperate and mesh with nature and with each other. A time when our homes will be built to last thousands of years and will be situated in a balanced relationship with our local ecosystems. Our science will be used to simplify our lives in a natural way that allows humanity and knowledge to progress to the next levels. Every person will be able to grow and work hard to express their full potential and give their gentle and loving gifts to the community of life. Everyone will live a satisfied life and will have riches far beyond anything materiality can provide.

The stars beckon us to explore the endless wonders which surround us. Gravity does not hold us prisoner upon the Earth, our ignorance does. If every person was given the opportunity to express their full potential, then the unique keys which they hold would unlock a bright future of unimaginable divine glory. There is nothing which we cannot attain, but there is a balanced path which we must follow.

I cannot say what that sacred future will look like. I know that from the time of the big bang and the initial flash of light which filled the universe with an intricately detailed vision; and the time when the first generations of stars formed the elements needed to create our bodies, that we were embedded with a spiritual purpose, a reason for being and for expanding our consciousness. Together we can become the essence of human potential and grow into a miraculous future.

Main Base Maria

The Plain of Deep Springs:
many robotic scouts
seek out the favorable place,
in proximity to variety.

The Plain of Deep Springs:
where the Martian desert
hides precious water underground,
the essential human resource.

The Plain of Deep Springs:
where lava tubes provide shelter
and access to deep resources,
rarest minerals and precious gems.

The Plain of Deep Springs:
Robots followed by peopled missions,
followed by commercial prospectors,
and soon by explorers and settlers.

The Plain of Deep Springs:
continually cannibalizing robots,
recycling everything left behind
in brilliant elegant simplicity.

The Plain of Deep Springs:
planetary outpost: shanty town Mars,
beyond hardships, loss, and grief,
boldly persevering and thriving.

The Plain of Deep Springs:
science, mining, and tourism,
glorious main base Maria,
the first step to the stars.

Gravitational Relativity

Heart of a Planet:
all Gravity pulling Out
see Duality

think outside the box
gravity faster than light
breathtaking vistas

Star Beacons calling
Super-string Entanglement
yearning for release

machine redesign
singularity promise
Dream Masters guiding

Metamorphosis
ships to interstellar crafts
gypsy migrations

all destinations
adventurous explorers
Winds carrying Seeds

colonies abound
flourishing on extreme Worlds
Love's Magic Power

Destiny Flower
fiery vacuum of thorns
New World Beauty Child

Epilog

what do you think?

more important:
what do you feel?

what are you doing
with your life?

what do you intend
to do
with your life?

I Love You!

I Bless you
upon your unique way
that only you
can choose...

www.ingramcontent.com/pod-product-compliance
Lightning Source LLC
Chambersburg PA
CBHW070641050426
42451CB00008B/257